C000230598

Messianic Prophecies Fulfilled in Jesus Christ

THOMAS NELSON PUBLISHERS

Published in Nashville, Tennessee by Thomas Nelson, Inc.

Unless otherwise indicated, Scripture quotations are from the *New King James Version of the Bible*, copyright © 1979, 1980, 1982, 1990, Thomas Nelson, Inc., Publishers.

Library of Congress Cataloging-in-Publication Data
Available from Library of Congress

Find It Fast: Messianic Prophecies Fulfilled in Jesus Christ
ISBN: 0-7852-4754-8

Printed in the United States of America
2 3 4 5—04 03 02

PROPHECIES SURROUNDING THE BIRTH OF CHRIST

Seed of a Woman

PROPHECY—GENESIS 3:15

> *And I will put enmity between you and the woman,*
> *and between your seed and her seed.*

FULFILLMENT—GALATIANS 4:4

Seed of Abraham

PROPHECY—GENESIS 12:3

> *I will bless those who bless you, and I will curse him*
> *who curses you; and in you all of the families of the*
> *earth shall be blessed.*

FULFILLMENT—MATTHEW 1:1; GALATIANS 3:8

Seed of Isaac

PROPHECY—GENESIS 17:19

> *Then God said: "No, Sarah your wife shall bear you a*
> *son, and you shall call his name Isaac; I will establish*
> *My covenant with him for an everlasting covenant, and*
> *with his descendants after him."*

FULFILLMENT—LUKE 3:34; GALATIANS 4:28

Seed of Jacob

PROPHECY—NUMBERS 24:17

> *"A Star shall come out of Jacob; a Scepter shall rise out*
> *of Israel."*

FULFILLMENT—MATTHEW 1:2

From the Tribe of Judah

PROPHECY—GENESIS 49:10

> *The scepter shall not depart from Judah.*

FULFILLMENT—LUKE 3:33

Heir to the Throne of David

PROPHECY—ISAIAH 9:7

> *Of the increase of His government and peace there will be no end, upon the throne of David and over His kingdom, to order it and establish it with judgment and justice.*

FULFILLMENT—LUKE 1:32, 33

Born in Bethlehem

PROPHECY—MICAH 5:2

> *"But you, Bethlehem Ephrathah, though you are little among the thousands of Judah, yet out of you shall come forth to Me The One to be Ruler in Israel."*

FULFILLMENT—LUKE 2:4-7

He Will Be Messiah

PROPHECY—DANIEL 9:25

> *Know therefore and understand, that from the going forth of the command to restore . . . Jerusalem until Messiah the Prince, there shall be seven weeks and sixty-two weeks.*

FULFILLMENT—JOHN 1:41; JOHN 4:25

To Be Born of a Virgin

PROPHECY—ISAIAH 7:14

> *Therefore the Lord Himself will give you a sign: Behold the virgin shall conceive and bear a Son.*

FULFILLMENT—LUKE 1:26-31

Immanuel, God with Us

PROPHECY—ISAIAH 7:14

> *And [you] shall call His name Immanuel.*

FULFILLMENT—MATTHEW 1:23

Slaughter of the Innocents

PROPHECY—JEREMIAH 31:15

> *Thus says the Lord: "A voice was heard in Ramah,
> lamentation and bitter weeping, Rachel weeping for her
> children, refusing to be comforted for her children,
> because they are no more."*

FULFILLMENT—MATTHEW 2:16-18

Flight to Egypt

PROPHECY—HOSEA 11:1

> *"When Israel was a child, I loved him, and out of Egypt
> I called My son."*

FULFILLMENT—MATTHEW 2:14-15

He Will Be Called a Nazarene

PROPHECY—JUDGES 13:5

> *"For behold, you shall conceive and bear a son. And no
> razor shall come upon his head, for the child shall be a
> Nazirite to God from the womb."*

FULFILLMENT—MATTHEW 2:23

PROPHECIES REGARDING CHRIST'S MINISTRY:

Preceded by a Forerunner

PROPHECY—MALACHI 3:1

> *"Behold, I send My messenger, and he will prepare the way before Me."*

FULFILLMENT—LUKE 7:24, 27

Preceded by a "Prophet Elijah"

PROPHECY—MALACHI 4:5

> *"Behold, I will send you Elijah the prophet before the coming of the great and dreadful day of the LORD."*

FULFILLMENT—LUKE 1:17

"A Voice Crying in the Wilderness"

PROPHECY—ISAIAH 40:3

> *"The voice of one crying in the wilderness: Prepare the way of the LORD; make straight in the desert a highway for our God."*

FULFILLMENT—MARK 1:2-3

Declared the Son of God

PROPHECY—PSALM 2:7

> *"I will declare the decree: the LORD has said to Me, 'You are My Son, today I have begotten You.'"*

FULFILLMENT—MATTHEW 3:17; MARK 9:7

The Spirit Is on Jesus

PROPHECY—ISAIAH 11:2

> *The Spirit of the LORD shall rest upon Him.*

FULFILLMENT—MATTHEW 3:16

God Is Pleased with Him

PROPHECY—ISAIAH 42:1

> *"Behold, My Servant whom I uphold, My Elect One in whom My soul delights!"*

FULFILLMENT—MARK 1:11

Angels Protect Him

PROPHECY—PSALM 91:11

> *For He shall give His angels charge over you, to keep you in all your ways.*

FULFILLMENT—MATTHEW 4:6

Galilean Ministry

PROPHECY—ISAIAH 9:1-2

> *By the way of the sea, beyond the Jordan, in Galilee of the Gentiles, the people who walked in darkness have seen a great light.*

FULFILLMENT—MATTHEW 4:13-16

Came to Teach the Jews

PROPHECY—PSALM 22:22

> *I will declare Your name to My brethren; in the midst of the assembly I will praise You.*

FULFILLMENT—MATTHEW 4:23-25

A Prophet

PROPHECY—DEUTERONOMY 18:15

> *"The LORD your God will raise up for you a Prophet like me from your midst."*

FULFILLMENT—ACTS 3:20-22

To Heal the Brokenhearted

PROPHECY—ISAIAH 61:1

> *"The Spirit of the Lord GOD is upon Me, because the LORD has anointed Me to preach good tidings to the poor; He has sent Me to heal the brokenhearted."*

FULFILLMENT—LUKE 4:18-19

Healing the Blind, Lame and Deaf

PROPHECY—ISAIAH 29:18

> *In that day the deaf shall hear the words of the book, and the eyes of the blind shall see out of . . . darkness.*

FULFILLMENT—MATTHEW 11:4-5

Rejected by His Own People, the Jews

PROPHECY—ISAIAH 53:3

> *He is despised and rejected by men, a Man of sorrows and acquainted with grief.*

FULFILLMENT—JOHN 1:11

Opposed by Hypocrites

PROPHECY—ISAIAH 29:13

> *"Inasmuch as these people draw near with their mouths and honor Me with their lips, but have removed their hearts far from Me."*

FULFILLMENT—MARK 7:6-8

Rulers Plot to Kill Him

PROPHECY—PSALM 2:2

> *The kings of the earth set themselves, and the rulers take counsel together, against the LORD and against His Anointed.*

FULFILLMENT—MARK 3:6

His Message Will Divide Families

PROPHECY—MICAH 7:6

> *For son dishonors father, daughter rises against her mother, daughter-in-law against her mother-in-law; a man's enemies are the men of his own household.*

FULFILLMENT—MATTHEW 10:35-36

Preaching in Parables

PROPHECY—PSALM 78:2

> *I will open my mouth in a parable; I will utter dark sayings of old.*

FULFILLMENT—MATTHEW 13:35

Priest after the Order of Melchizedek

PROPHECY—PSALM 110:4

> *The LORD has sworn and will not relent, You are a priest forever according to the order of Melchizedek.*

FULFILLMENT—HEBREWS 5:5-6

He Is the Cornerstone

PROPHECY—PSALM 118:22

> *The stone which the builders rejected has become the chief cornerstone.*

FULFILLMENT—MATTHEW 21:42

PROPHECIES REGARDING HIS DEATH:

Riding on a Donkey

PROPHECY—ZECHARIAH 9:9

"Rejoice greatly, O daugher of Zion! Shout O daughter of Jerusalem! Behold, your King is coming to you; He is just and having salvation, lowly and riding on a donkey, a colt, the foal of a donkey."

FULFILLMENT—MARK 11:7-11

Shouts of Hosanna

PROPHECY—PSALM 118:25-26

Save now, I pray, O LORD; O LORD, I pray, send now prosperity. Blessed is he who comes in the name of the LORD!

FULFILLMENT—MATTHEW 21:4

Children Call Out His Praises

PROPHECY—PSALM 8:2

Out of the mouth babes and nursing infants you have ordained strength, because of Your enemies, that You may silence the enemy and the avenger.

FULFILLMENT—MATTHEW 21:16

Driving Out the Money-Changers

PROPHECY—MALACHI 3:1

"And the Lord, whom you seek, will suddenly come to His temple."

FULFILLMENT—MATTHEW 21:12-13

Betrayed by a Friend

PROPHECY—PSALM 41:9

> *Even my own familiar friend in whom I trusted, who ate my bread, has lifted up his heel against me.*

FULFILLMENT—LUKE 22:47-48

Sold for Thirty Pieces of Silver

PROPHECY—ZECHARIAH 11:12

> *"If it is agreeable to you, give me my wages; and if not, refrain." So they weighed out for my wages thirty pieces of silver.*

FULFILLMENT—MATTHEW 26:15

Abandoned by the Disciples

PROPHECY—ZECHARIAH 13:7

> *"Strike the Shepherd, and the sheep will be scattered; then I will turn My hand against the little ones."*

FULFILLMENT—MATTHEW 26:31

"Your Will Be done"

PROPHECY—ISAIAH 50:5

> *The Lord GOD has opened My ear, and I was not rebellious, nor did I turn away.*

FULFILLMENT—MATTHEW 26:42

Accused by False Witnesses

PROPHECY—PSALM 35:11

> *Fierce witnesses rise up.*

FULFILLMENT—MARK 14:57-58

Silent to Accusations

PROPHECY—ISAIAH 53:7

> *He was oppressed and He was afflicted, yet He opened not His mouth.*

FULFILLMENT—MARK 15:4-5

Beaten

PROPHECY—ISAIAH 50:6

> *"I gave My back to those who struck Me, and My cheeks to those who plucked out the beard."*

FULFILLMENT—MATTHEW 26:67

Whipped

PROPHECY—ISAIAH 53:5

> *But He was wounded for our transgressions, He was bruised for our iniquities; the chastisement for our peace was upon Him, and by His stripes we are healed.*

FULFILLMENT—MATTHEW 27:26

Mocked and Spit Upon

PROPHECY—ISAIAH 50:6

> *"I did not hide My face from shame and spitting."*

FULFILLMENT—MATTHEW 27:29-30

Struck in the Face with a Rod

PROPHECY—MICAH 5:1

> *They will strike the judge of Israel with a rod on the cheek.*

FULFILLMENT—MARK 15:19

Hated without Reason

PROPHECY—PSALM 35:19

> *Let them not rejoice over me who are wrongfully my enemies; Nor let them wink with the eye who hate me without a cause.*

FULFILLMENT—JOHN 15:24-25

The Rooster Crows

PROPHECY—MATTHEW 26:34

> *Jesus said to him, "Assuredly, I say to you that this night, before the rooster crows, you will deny Me three times."*

FULFILLMENT—MATTHEW 26:74-75

Vicarious Sacrifice

PROPHECY—ISAIAH 53:5

> *The chastisement for our peace was upon Him.*

FULFILLMENT—ROMANS 5:6, 8

His Life Will Ransom Many

PROPHECY—ISAIAH 53:10

> *When You make His soul an offering for sin, He shall see His seed, He shall prolong His days.*

FULFILLMENT—MATTHEW 20:28; ACTS 2:24

Crucified with Thieves

PROPHECY—ISAIAH 53:12

> *And He was numbered with the transgressors, and He bore the sin of many, and made intercession for the transgressors.*

FULFILLMENT—MARK 15:27-28

Pierced Through Hands and Feet

PROPHECY—ZECHARIAH 12:10

> *"And I will pour on the house of David and on the inhabitants of Jerusalem the Spirit of grace and supplication; then they will look on Me whom they pierced. Yes, they will mourn for Him as one mourns for his only son, and grieve for Him as one grieves for a firstborn."*

FULFILLMENT—JOHN 20:27

Scorned and Mocked by His Captors

PROPHECY—PSALM 22:7-8

> *All those who see Me ridicule Me; they shoot out the lip, they shake the head, saying, "He trusted in the LORD, let Him rescue Him."*

FULFILLMENT—LUKE 23:35

Passersby Shake Their Heads and Mock

PROPHECY—PSALM 109:25

> *I also have become a reproach to them; when they look at me, they shake their heads.*

FULFILLMENT—MATTHEW 27:39

Given Vinegar and Gall

PROPHECY—PSALM 69:21

> *They also gave me gall for my food, and for my thirst they gave me vinegar to drink.*

FULFILLMENT—MATTHEW 27:34

Prayer for His Enemies

PROPHECY—PSALM 109:4

> *In return for my love they are my accusers, but I give myself to prayer.*

FULFILLMENT—LUKE 23:34

Soldiers Gambled for His Coat

PROPHECY—PSALM 22:17-18

> *I can count all My bones. They look and stare at Me. They divide My garments among them, and for My clothing they cast lots.*

FULFILLMENT—MATTHEW 27:35-36

No Bones Broken

PROPHECY—PSALM 34:20

> *He guards all his bones; not one of them is broken.*

FULFILLMENT—JOHN 19:32-36

His Side Pierced

PROPHECY—ZECHARIAH 12:10

> *"And I will pour on the house of David and on the inhabitants of Jerusalem the Spirit of grace and supplication; then they will look on Me whom they*

> *pierced. Yes, they will mourn for Him as one mourns for his only son, and grieve for Him as one grieves for a firstborn."*

FULFILLMENT—JOHN 19:34

God Forsakes Jesus

PROPHECY—PSALM 22:1

> *My God, My God, why have You forsaken Me?*

FULFILLMENT—MATTHEW 27:46

Temple Curtain Torn in Two

PROPHECY—ZECHARIAH 11:10-11

> *And I took My staff, Beauty, and cut it in two, that I might break the covenant which I had made with all the peoples.*

FULFILLMENT—MATTHEW 27:51

Darkness Fell

PROPHECY—AMOS 8:9

> *"And it shall come to pass in that day," says the Lord GOD, "That I will make the sun go down at noon, and I will darken the earth in broad daylight."*

FULFILLMENT—MARK 15:33

Anointed for Burial

PROPHECY—MARK 14:8

> *"She has done what she could. She has come beforehand to anoint My body for burial."*

FULFILLMENT—JOHN 19:40-42

Buried with the Rich

PROPHECY—ISAIAH 53:9

> *And they made His grave with the wicked—but with the rich at His death.*

FULFILLMENT—MATTHEW 27:57-60

To Be Resurrected

PROPHECY—PSALM 16:10

> For You will not leave my soul in Sheol, nor will You allow Your Holy One to see corruption.

FULFILLMENT—MARK 16:6-7

Raised after Three Days

PROPHECY—HOSEA 6:2

> After two days He will revive us; On the third day He will raise us up, that we may live in His sight.

FULFILLMENT—1 CORINTHIANS 15:4; JOHN 20:1

His Ascension to God's Right Hand

PROPHECY—PSALM 68:18

> You have ascended on high, You have led captivity captive.

FULFILLMENT—MARK 16:19